Keto Chaffle Recipes Cookbook

Satisfying and Flagrant Recipes to Loss Weight and Maximize your Energy

Reyhan Hoque

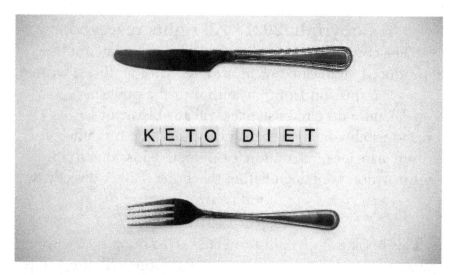

TABLE OF CONTENTS

INTRODUCTION

A chaffle, or cheese waffle, is an egg and cheese keto waffle. Chaffles become a popular snack of keto / low-carb. Chaffle is made with coconut and pumpkin, making it a healthy low-carb alternative for anyone looking to lose weight. The chaffle helps stabilize blood sugar levels so the body has an easier time sensing when food is needed. The keto chaffle contains no calories or carbs, making it an ideal tool for anyone looking to lose or maintain their weight.

What is this keto Chaffle recipe in the world that has overtaken and conquered the keto community? Simply put, it's a cheese and egg waffle. There have been various variants in Facebook groups since the original recipe came out

How to make crispy chaffle

First off, beat one egg in a mixing bowl until you achieve the desired consistency and add ½ cup of finely shredded mozzarella cheese. Preheat the mini waffle iron then pour the mixture into it

If you find the taste too eggy, you can add a tablespoon of almond flour or any keto-friendly flour like coconut flour, psyllium husk flour, ground flax seed and the like. You can also top it with sugar free syrup and butter.

You can also try other kinds of cheese to see what will make your taste buds happier.

If you want it crunchier, you have to sprinkle shredded cheese on the waffle maker first and let it melt for half a minute before adding the mixture.

This is just the classic chaffle though. Remember that you can be creative with it and possibilities are endless!

Chaffles can be used for hamburger bun, hotdog bun, sandwich and pizza crust. You can also make it sweet or savory.

11 Tips to Make Chaffles

- **Preheat Well:** Yes! It sounds obvious to preheat the waffle iron before usage. However, preheating the iron moderately will not get your chaffles as crispy as you will like. The best way to preheat before cooking is to ensure that the iron is very hot.

- **Not-So-Cheesy:** Will you prefer to have your chaffles less cheesy? Then, use mozzarella cheese.

- **Not-So Eggy**: If you aren't comfortable with the smell of eggs in your chaffles, try using egg whites instead of egg yolks or whole eggs.

- **To Shred or to Slice:** Many recipes call for shredded cheese when making chaffles, but I find sliced cheeses to offer crispier pieces. While I stick with mostly shredded cheese for convenience's sake, be at ease to use sliced cheese in the same quantity. When using sliced cheeses, arrange two to four pieces in the waffle iron, top with the beaten eggs, and some slices of the cheese. Cover and cook until crispy.

- **Shallower Irons:** For better crisps on your chaffles, use shallower waffle irons as they cook easier and faster.

- **Layering:** Don't fill up the waffle iron with too much batter. Work between a quarter and a half cup of total ingredients per batch for correctly done chaffles.

- **Patience:** It is a virtue even when making chaffles. For the best results, allow the chaffles to sit in the iron for 5 to 7 minutes before serving.

- **No Peeking:** 7 minutes isn't too much of a time to wait for the outcome of your chaffles, in my opinion. Opening the iron and checking on the chaffle before it is done stands you a worse chance of ruining it.

- **Crispy Cooling:** For better crisp, I find that allowing the chaffles to cool further after they are transferred to a plate aids a lot.

- **Easy Cleaning:** For the best cleanup, wet a paper towel and wipe the inner parts of the iron clean while still warm. Kindly note that the iron should be warm but not hot!

- **Brush It:** Also, use a clean toothbrush to clean between the iron's teeth for a thorough cleanup. You may also use a dry, rough sponge to clean the iron while it is still warm

CHAPTER 1:

BREAKFAST CHAFFLE

RECIPES

1. Mini Breakfast Chaffles

Difficulty level: Medium

Preparation Time: 10 minutes

Servings: 3

Cooking Time: 15 Minutes

Ingredients:

- 6 tsp coconut flour

- 1 tsp stevia

- 1/4 tsp baking powder

- 2 eggs

- 3 oz. cream cheese

- 1/2. tsp vanilla extract

- Topping

- 1 egg

- 6 slice bacon

- 2 oz. Raspberries for topping

- 2 oz. Blueberries for topping

- 2 oz. Strawberries for topping

Directions:

1. Heat up your square waffle maker and grease with cooking spray.

2. Mix together coconut flour, stevia, egg, baking powder, cheese and vanilla in mixing bowl.

3. Pour ½ of chaffles mixture in a waffle maker.

4. Close the lid and cook the chaffles for about 3-5 minutes Utes.

5. Meanwhile, fry bacon slices in pan on medium heat for about 2-3 minutes Utes until cooked and transfer them to plate.

6. In the same pan, fry eggs one by one in the leftover grease of bacon.

7. Once chaffles are cooked, carefully transfer them to plate.

8. Serve with fried eggs and bacon slice and berries on top.

9. Enjoy!

Nutrition: Protein: 16% 75 kcal Fat: 75% 346 kcal Carbohydrates: 9% 41 kcal

2. <u>**Morning Chaffles With Berries**</u>

Difficulty level: Easy **Preparation Time:** 10 minutes

Servings: 4 **Cooking Time:** 5 Minutes

Ingredients:

- 1 cup egg whites

- 1 cup cheddar cheese, shredded

- ¼ cup almond flour

- ¼ cup heavy cream

- TOPPING

- 4 oz. raspberries

- 4 oz. strawberries.

- 1 oz. keto chocolate flakes

- 1 oz. feta cheese.

Directions:

1. Preheat your square waffle maker and grease with cooking spray.

2. Beat egg white in a small bowl with flour.

3. Add shredded cheese to the egg whites and flour mixture and mix well.

4. Add cream and cheese to the egg mixture.

5. Pour Chaffles batter in a waffle maker and close the lid.

6. Cook chaffles for about 4 minutes Utes until crispy and brown.

7. Carefully remove chaffles from the maker. Serve with berries, cheese, and chocolate on top. Enjoy!

Nutrition: Protein: 28% 68 kcal Fat: 67% 163 kcal Carbohydrates: 5% 12 kcal

3. <u>Hot Dog Chaffles</u>

Difficulty level: Medium

Preparation Time: 15 minutes

Cooking Time: 14 minutes

Servings: 2

Ingredients:

- 1 egg, beaten

- 1 cup finely grated cheddar cheese

- 2 hot dog sausages, cooked

- Mustard dressing for topping

- 8 pickle slices

Directions:

1. Preheat the waffle iron.

2. In a medium bowl, mix the egg and cheddar cheese.

3. Open the iron and add half of the mixture. Close and cook until crispy, 7 minutes.

4. Transfer the chaffle to a plate and make a second chaffle in the same manner.

5. To serve, top each chaffle with a sausage, swirl the mustard dressing on top, and then divide the pickle slices on top.

6. Enjoy!

Nutrition: Calories: 231 Cal Total Fat: 18.29 g Saturated Fat: 0 g Cholesterol: 0 mg Sodium: 0 mg Total Carbs: 2.8 g Fiber: 0 g Sugar: 0 g Protein: 13.39 g

4. <u>Crispy Chaffles With Sausage</u>

Difficulty level: Medium **Preparation Time:** 10 minutes

Servings: 2 **Cooking Time:** 10 Minutes

Ingredients:

- 1/2 cup cheddar cheese
- 1/2 tsp. baking powder
- 1/4 cup egg whites
- 2 tsp. pumpkin spice
- 1 egg, whole
- 2 chicken sausage
- 2 slice bacon
- salt and pepper to taste
- 1 tsp. avocado oil

Directions:

1. Mix together all ingredients in a bowl.
2. Allow batter to sit while waffle iron warms.

3. Spray waffle iron with nonstick spray.

4. Pour batter in the waffle maker and cook according to the directions of the manufacturer.

5. Meanwhile, heat oil in a pan and fry the egg, according to your choice and transfer it to plate.

6. In the same pan, fry bacon slice and sausage on medium heat for about 2-3 minutes Utes until cooked.

7. Once chaffles are cooked thoroughly, remove them from the maker.

8. Serve with fried egg, bacon slice, sausages and enjoy!

Nutrition: Protein: 22% 86 kcal Fat: 74% 286 kcal Carbohydrates: 3% 12 kcal

5. <u>Chili Chaffle</u>

Difficulty level: Medium

Preparation Time: 10 minutes

Servings: 4

Cooking Time: 7–9 Minutes

Ingredients:

- Batter

- 4 eggs

- ½ cup grated parmesan cheese

- 1½ cups grated yellow cheddar cheese

- 1 hot red chili pepper

- Salt and pepper to taste

- ½ teaspoon dried garlic powder

- 1 teaspoon dried basil

- 2 tablespoons almond flour

- Other

- 2 tablespoons olive oil for brushing the waffle maker

Directions:

1. Preheat the waffle maker.

2. Crack the eggs into a bowl and add the grated parmesan and cheddar cheese.

3. Mix until just combined and add the chopped chili pepper. Season with salt and pepper, dried garlic powder and dried basil. Stir in the almond flour.

4. Mix until everything is combined.

5. Brush the heated waffle maker with olive oil and add a few tablespoons of the batter.

6. Close the lid and cook for about 7–8 minutes depending on your waffle maker.

Nutrition: Calories 36 fat 30.4 g, carbs 3.1 g, sugar 0.7 g, Protein 21.5 g, sodium 469 mg

6. <u>Egg On A Cheddar Cheese Chaffle</u>

Preparation Time: 10 minutes

Difficulty level: Medium

Servings: 4

Cooking Time: 7–9 Minutes

Ingredients:

- Batter

- 4 eggs

- 2 cups shredded white cheddar cheese

- Salt and pepper to taste

- Other

- 2 tablespoons butter for brushing the waffle maker 4 large eggs

- 2 tablespoons olive oil

Directions:

1. Preheat the waffle maker.

2. Crack the eggs into a bowl and whisk them with a fork.

3. Stir in the grated cheddar cheese and season with salt and pepper.

4. Brush the heated waffle maker with butter and add a few tablespoons of the batter. Close the lid and cook for about 7–8 minutes depending on your waffle maker.

5. While chaffles are cooking, cook the eggs. Warm the oil in a large non-stick pan that has a lid over medium-low heat for 2-3 minutes

6. Crack an egg in a small ramekin and gently add it to the pan. Repeat the same way for the other 3 eggs.

7. Cover and let cook for 2 to 2 ½ minutes for set eggs but with runny yolks. Remove from heat.

8. To serve, place a chaffle on each plate and top with an egg. Season with salt and black pepper to taste.

Nutrition: Calories 4 fat 34 g, carbs 2 g, sugar 0.6 g, Protein 26 g, sodium 518 mg

CHAPTER 2:

LUNCH CHAFFLE RECIPES

7. <u>Blt Chaffle</u>

Preparation Time: 30 minutes

Difficulty level: Hard

Cooking Time: 40 Minutes

Servings: 1 large chaffles or 2 mini chaffles

Ingredients

Blt ingredients

- 1 tbsp of mayonnaise

- 1 handful of lettuce, shredded

- 1 slice of an heirloom tomato

- 2 slices of bacon

Tools: waffle maker, mini or regular sized, one mixing bowl, measuring cups and tablespoons, spatula, non-stick cooking spray (or butter), saucepan, blender, electric beaters, or whisk.

Directions

1. Shred the lettuce and slice the tomatoes.

2. Take a medium-sized pan and put on medium heat.

3. Take the bacon and cook until desired texture, chewy or crunchy.

4. Set aside when done.

5. Follow the classic chaffle recipe.

6. Once the chaffles are done, lay two chaffles side by side.

7. Layer on the mayonnaise, bacon, lettuce, and tomatoes.

8. Enjoy!

Nutrition: Calories 366, Carbs 6 g, Fat 19 g, Protein 43 g, Sodium 1183 mg, Sugar 0 g

8. <u>Cajun Shrimp And Avocado Chaffle</u>

Difficulty level: Easy

Preparation Time: 15 minutes

Cooking Time: 10 minutes

Servings: 2

Ingredients to Use:

- 2 slices of bacon

- 1/2 cup cheddar cheese (shredded)

- 1 Tbsp. Avocado oil

- 1 egg

- 1/2 cup of onions (sliced)

- 2 tsp. Cajun seasoning

- 1 Tbsp. Almond flour

- 1 lb. Shrimps

- Salt and pepper to taste

Step-by-Step Directions to cook it:

1. Heat avocado oil in a pan placed over low-medium heat. Add the bacon and cook for 3 minutes per side or until crispy brown. Remove from the pieces from the

2. Oil and pat dry with a paper towel. Set aside the oil used.

3. Put the shrimp in a bowl, add Cajun seasoning, avocado oil, salt, and pepper. Allow it to marinate for 15 minutes. Place the used oil on medium heat and fry the shrimp for 2 minutes per side. Remove and dry with a paper towel.

4. To make the chaffle bread, preheat the waffle machine. In a bowl, combine egg, cheddar cheese,

almond flour, and Cajun seasoning. Cook in your

waffle machine.

5. Assemble your sandwich and serve.

Nutrition: Calorie: 390kcal, Carbs: 2.5g, Fats: 16g, Protein:

19g

9. <u>Keto Chocolate Chaffle</u>

Chocolate chaffle is a combination of three different flavors. It is sweet and tasty, just the perfect meal for a nice breakfast or late lunch.

Difficulty level: Easy

Preparation Time: 5 minutes

Cooking Time: 15 minutes

Servings: 2

Ingredients to Use:

- 1 tsp vanilla extract - 1 egg

- 1 tsp of cocoa powder

- 3/4 oz. Cream cheese

- 1-1/2 Tbsp coconut flour

Step-by-Step Directions to cook it:

1. In a bowl, add all the ingredients and mix thoroughly.

2. Preheat the waffle-maker, pour the mixture and allow to cook for 3-4minutes or until it turns golden brown. Serve hot.

Nutrition: Calorie: 230kcal, Carbs: 4g, Fats: 10g, Protein: 13g

CHAPTER 3:

DINNER CHAFFLES

10. Vegan Keto Chaffle Waffle

Preparation timetime: 10 minutes

Difficulty level: EASY

Cooking Time: 5 minutes

Servings: 2

Ingredients

- 1 tablespoon flax seed

- 2 glasses of water

- ¼ cup low carb vegan cheese

- 22 tablespoons coconut powder

- 1 1 tbsp low carb vegan cream cheese

- A pinch of salt

Directions

1. Preheat the waffle maker to medium high heat.

2. In a small bowl, mix flax seed meal and water. Leave for 5 minutes until thick and sticky.

3. Make flax eggs

4. Whisk all vegan chaffle ingredients together. Meat vegan keto waffle

5. Pour vegan waffle dough into the center of the waffle iron.

6. Close the waffle maker and cook for 3-5 minutes or until the waffles are golden and firm. If using a mini waffle maker, pour only half the dough. Pour the waffle mixture into the waffle maker

7. Remove the vegan chaffle from the waffle maker and serve.

8. You can eat vegan keto chaffles

Nutrition: Calories 168, total Fat 11.8g, cholesterol 121mg, sodium 221.8mg, total carbohydrate 5.1g, dietary Fiber 1.7g, sugars 1.2g, Protein 10g, vitamin a 133.5μg, vitamin c 7.3mg

CHAPTER 4:

CHAFFLE CAKE &

SANDWICH RECIPES

11. Fluffy White Chaffles

Difficulty level: Easy **Preparation time:** 10 minutes

Cooking time: 5 minutes **Servings:** 4 mini chaffles

Ingredients:

- 1 large egg 1 large egg white

- 2 tablespoons cream cheese

- ½ cup grated Mozzarella cheese

- 2 tablespoons coconut flour

- ¼ cup almond flour

- ¼ teaspoon vanilla extract

- ½ teaspoon baking powder ¼ cup Swerve

Directions:

1. Preheat the mini waffle maker.

2. Place the egg, egg white, cream cheese, and Mozzarella into a blender. Process until smooth. Add the remaining ingredients and process again.

3. Spoon one quarter of the batter into the waffle maker. Cooking for 2 to 4 minutes or until golden brown. Transfer the chaffle onto a cooling rack to cool. Repeat with the remaining batter.

4. Serve immediately.

Nutrition: Calories 1 Total Fat 12.5g Saturated Fat 7g Cholesterol 112mg Sodium267mg Total Carbohydrate 4.9g Dietary Fiber 0.1g Total Sugars 2.7g Protein 12g Potassium 73mg

12. Blueberry Keto Chaffle

Difficulty level: Easy

Preparation time: 3 minutes

Cooking time: 15 minutes

Servings: 5

Ingredients:

- 2 eggs

- 1 cup Mozzarella cheese

- 2 tablespoons almond flour

- 2 teaspoons Swerve, plus additional for serving

- 1 teaspoon baking powder

- 1 teaspoon cinnamon

- 3 tablespoon blueberries

- Nonstick cooking spray

Directions:

1. Preheat the mini waffle maker.

2. Stir together the eggs, Mozzarella cheese, almond flour, Swerve, baking powder, cinnamon, and blueberries in a mixing bowl. Spray the waffle maker with nonstick cooking spray.

3. Pour in a little bit less than ¼ a cup of blueberry waffle batter at a time.

4. Close the lid and cooking the chaffle for 3 to 5 minutes. Check it at the 3-minute mark to see if it is crispy and brown. If it is not or it sticks to the top of the waffle maker, close the lid and cooking for an additional 1 to 2 minutes.

5. Serve sprinkled with additional Swerve.

Nutrition: **(per serving):**Calories: 10cal ;Carbohydrates:5g ;Protein: 7g;Fat: 7g ;Saturated Fat:4g ;Cholesterol:97mg ;Sodium:132mg ;Potassium: 176mg ;Fiber: 3g ;Sugar: 1g ;Vitamin A: 255IU ;Calcium: 121mg ;Iron: 1mg

13. Keto Birthday Cake Chaffle Recipe With Sprinkles

Difficulty level: Easy

Preparation Time: 10 minutes

Cooking Time: 7 minutes   **Servings:** 4

Ingredients:

Ingredients for chaffle cake:

- 2 eggs

- 1/4 almond flour

- 1 cup coconut powder

- 1 cup melted butter

- 2 tablespoons cream cheese

- 1 teaspoon cake butter extract

- 1 tsp. vanilla extract

- 2 tsp. baking powder

- 2 teaspoons confectionery sweetener or monk fruit

- 1/4 teaspoon xanthan powder whipped cream

Vanilla frosting ingredients

- 1/2 cup heavy whipped cream

- 2 tablespoons sweetener or monk fruit

- 1/2 teaspoon vanilla extract

Directions:

1. The mini waffle maker is preheated.

2. Add all the ingredients of the chaffle cake in a medium-sized blender and blend it to the top until it is smooth and creamy. Allow only a minute to sit with the batter. It may seem a little watery, but it's going to work well.

3. Add 2 to 3 tablespoons of batter to your waffle maker and cooking until golden brown for about 2 to 3 minutes.

4. Start to frost the whipped vanilla cream in a separate bowl.

5. Add all the ingredients and mix with a hand mixer until thick and soft peaks are formed by the whipping cream.

6. Until frosting your cake, allow the cake to cool completely. If you frost it too soon, the frosting will be melted.

7. Enjoy!

Nutrition: Calories 179Fat 14.5 carbohydrates 1.9 sugar 0.4 protein 10.8 cholesterol 19mg

CHAPTER 5:

VEGETARIAN CHAFFLE

RECIPES

14.Cinnamon Cream Cheese Chaffle

Preparation time: 10 minutes

Difficulty level: Hard

Cooking Time: 15 Minutes

Servings: 2

Ingredients:

- 2 eggs, lightly beaten

- 1 tsp collagen

- ¼ tsp baking powder, gluten-free

- 1 tsp monk fruit sweetener

- ½ tsp cinnamon

- ¼ cup cream cheese, softened

- Pinch of salt

Directions:

1. Preheat your waffle maker.

2. Add all ingredients into the bowl and beat using hand mixer until well combined.

3. Spray waffle maker with cooking spray.

4. Pour 1/2 batter in the hot waffle maker and cook for 3-minutes or until golden brown. Repeat with the remaining batter.

5. Serve and enjoy.

Nutrition: Calories 179Fat 14.5 carbohydrates 1.9 sugar 0.4 protein 10.8 cholesterol 19mg

CHAPTER 6:

BASIC CHAFFLES RECIPES

15. Basic Mozzarella Chaffles

Preparation time: 10 minutes

Difficulty level: Medium

Cooking Time: 6 Minutes **Servings:** 2

Ingredients:

- 1 large organic egg, beaten

- ½ cup Mozzarella cheese, shredded finely

Directions:

1. Preheat a mini waffle iron and then grease it. In a small bowl, place the egg and Mozzarella cheese

and stir to combine. Place half of the mixture into preheated waffle iron and cook for about 2-minutes or until golden brown.

2. Repeat with the remaining mixture.

3. Serve warm.

Nutrition: Calories: 5Net Carb: 0.4g Fat: 3.7g Saturated Fat: 1.5g Carbohydrates: 0.4g Dietary Fiber: 0g Sugar: 0.2g Protein: 5.2g

16. Basic Keto Chaffle Recipe

Difficulty level: Medium

Preparation Time: 5 minutes

Cooking Time: 8 minutes **Servings:** 1

Ingredients:

- 1 egg

- 1/2 cup cheddar cheese, shredded

1. Turn waffle maker on or plug it in so that it heats and grease both sides.

2. In a small bowl, crack an egg, then add the 1/2 cup cheddar cheese and stir to combine.

Pour 1

Directions:

3. /2 of the batter in the waffle maker and close the top.

4. Cooking for 3-4 minutes or until it reaches desired doneness.

5. Carefully remove from waffle maker and set aside for 2-3 minutes to give it time to crisp.

6. Follow the Directions again to make the second chaffle.

Nutrition: Total Calories 401 kcal Fats 219 g Protein 32.35 g Nectars 1.46 g Fiber 3 g

17.Cinnamon Keto Chaffles

Preparation Time: 5 minutes

Difficulty level: Medium

Cooking Time: 10 minutes

Servings: 3

Ingredients:

- 1/2 cup Mozzarella cheese

- 1 tablespoon almond flour

- 1/4 tsp. baking powder

- 1 egg

- 1 tsp. cinnamon

- 1 tsp. Granulated Swerve

- Cinnamon roll swirl Ingredients:

- 1 tbsp. butter

- 1 tsp. cinnamon

- 2 tsp. confectioner's swerve

- Keto Cinnamon Roll Glaze

- 1 tablespoon butter

- 1 tablespoon cream cheese

- 1/4 tsp. vanilla extract

- 2 tsp. swerve confectioners

Directions:

1. Plug in your Mini Dash Waffle maker and let it heat up.

2. In a small bowl mix the Mozzarella cheese, almond flour, baking powder, egg, 1 teaspoon cinnamon, and 1 teaspoon swerve granulated and set aside.

3. In another small bowl, add a tablespoon of butter, 1 teaspoon cinnamon, and 2 teaspoons of swerve confectioners' sweetener.

4. Microwave for 15 seconds and mix well.

5. Spray the waffle maker with nonstick spray and add 1/3 of the batter to your waffle maker. Swirl in 1/3 of the cinnamon, swerve, and butter mixture onto the top of it. Close the waffle maker and let cooking for 3-4 minutes.

6. When the first cinnamon roll chaffle is done, make the second and then make the third.

7. While the third chaffle is cooking place 1 tablespoon butter and 1 tablespoon of cream cheese in a small bowl. Heat in the microwave for 10-15 seconds. Start at 10, and if the cream cheese is not soft enough to mix with the butter heat for an additional 5 seconds.

8. Add the vanilla extract, and the swerve confectioner's sweetener to the butter and cream cheese and mix well using a whisk.

9. Drizzle keto cream cheese glaze on top of chaffle.

Nutrition: Calories 171Total Fat 10.7g Saturated Fat5.3g Cholesterol97mg Sodium106mg Potassium 179mgTotal Carbohydrate 3g Dietary Fiber 4. Protein 5.8g Total Sugars 0.4g

18.Keto Chaffle Breakfast Sandwich

Preparation Time: 3 minutes

Difficulty level: Medium

Cooking Time: 6 minutes **Servings:** 1

Ingredients:

- 1 egg

- 1/2 cup Monterey Jack Cheese

- 1 tablespoon almond flour

- 2 tablespoons butter

Directions:

1. In a small bowl, mix the egg, almond flour, and Monterey Jack Cheese.

2. Pour half of the batter into your mini waffle maker and cooking for 3-4 minutes. Then cooking the rest of the batter to make a second chaffle.

3. In a small pan, melt 2 tablespoons of butter. Add the chaffles and cooking on each side for 2 minutes. Pressing down while they are cooking lightly on the top of them, so they crisp up better.

4. Remove from the pan and let sit for 2 minutes.

Nutrition: Calories 170Total Fat 13 g Saturated Fat 7 g Cholesterol 112 mg Sodium 211 mg Potassium 94 mg Total Carbohydrate 2 g Dietary Fiber 1 g Protein 11 g Total Sugars 1 g

CHAPTER 7:

SWEET CHAFFLES RECIPES

19. Blueberry Cinnamon Chaffles

Preparation time: 5 minutes **Difficulty level:** Easy

Servings: 3 **Cooking Time:** 10 Minutes

Ingredients:

- 1 cup shredded mozzarella cheese

- 3 Tbsp almond flour

- 2 eggs

- 2 tsp Swerve or granulated sweetener of choice

- 1 tsp cinnamon

- ½ tsp baking powder

- ½ cup fresh blueberries

- ½ tsp of powdered Swerve

Directions:

1. Turn on waffle maker to heat and oil it with cooking spray.

2. Mix eggs, flour, mozzarella, cinnamon, vanilla extract, sweetener, and baking powder in a bowl until well combined.

3. Add in blueberries.

4. Pour ¼ batter into each waffle mold.

5. Close and cook for 8 minutes.

6. If it's crispy and the waffle maker opens without pulling the chaffles apart, the chaffle is ready. If not, close and cook for 1-2 minutes more.

7. Serve with favorite topping and more blueberries.

Nutrition: Carbs: 9 g ;Fat: 12 g ;Protein: 13 g ;Calories: 193

20. <u>Chocolate Chaffles</u>

Preparation time: 5 minutes   **Difficulty level:** Easy

Cooking Time: 10 Minutes

Servings: 2

Ingredients:

- ¾ cup shredded mozzarella

- 1 large egg 2 Tbsp almond flour

- 2 Tbsp allulose

- ½ Tbsp melted butter

- 1½ Tbsp cocoa powder

- ½ tsp vanilla extract

- ½ tsp psyllium husk powder

- ¼ tsp baking powder

Directions:

1. Turn on waffle maker to heat and oil it with cooking spray.

2. Mix all ingredients in a small bowl.

3. Pour ¼ cup batter into a 4-inch waffle maker. Cook for 2-3 minutes, or until crispy. Transfer chaffle to a plate and set aside.

4. Repeat with remaining batter.

Nutrition: Carbs: 6 g ;Fat: 24 g ;Protein: 15 g ;Calories: 296

21. Churro Waffles

Preparation time: 5 minutes **Difficulty level:** Easy

Servings: 1 **Cooking Time:** 10 Minutes

Ingredients:

- 1 tbsp coconut cream

- 1 egg

- 6 tbsp almond flour

- ¼ tsp xanthan gum

- ½ tsp cinnamon

- 2 tbsp keto brown sugar

- Coating: 2 tbsp butter, melt

- 1 tbsp keto brown sugar

- Warm up your waffle maker.

Directions:

1. Pour half of the batter to the waffle pan and cook for 5 minutes.

2. Carefully remove the cooked waffle and repeat the steps with the remaining batter.

3. Allow the chaffles to cool and spread with the melted butter and top with the brown sugar.

4. Enjoy.

Nutrition: Calories per Servings: 178 Kcal,Fats: 15.7 g ,Carbs: 3.9 g ,Protein: 2 g

22. Banana Nut Chaffle

Preparation time: 5 minutes

Difficulty level: Easy

Servings: 1

Cooking Time: 10 Minutes

Ingredients:

- 1 egg

- 1 Tbsp cream cheese, softened and room temp

- 1 Tbsp sugar-free cheesecake pudding

- ½ cup mozzarella cheese

- 1 Tbsp monk fruit confectioners' sweetener

- ¼ tsp vanilla extract

- ¼ tsp banana extract toppings of choice

Directions:

1. Turn on waffle maker to heat and oil it with cooking spray.

2. Beat egg in a small bowl.

3. Add remaining ingredients and mix until well incorporated.

4. Add one half of the batter to waffle maker and cook for minutes, until golden brown.

5. Remove chaffle and add the other half of the batter.

6. Top with your optional toppings and serve warm!

Nutrition: Carbs: 2 g ;Fat: g ;Protein: 8 g ;Calories: 119

23. Chocolate Chips Lemon Chaffles

Preparation time: 8 minutes   **Cooking Time:** 8 Minutes

Difficulty level: Easy

Servings: 2

Ingredients:

- 2 organic eggs

- ½ cup Mozzarella cheese, shredded

- ¾ teaspoon organic lemon extract

- ½ teaspoon organic vanilla extract

- 2 teaspoons Erythritol

- ½ teaspoon psyllium husk powder

- Pinch of salt

- 1 tablespoon 70% dark chocolate chips

- ¼ teaspoon lemon zest, grated finely

Directions:

1. Preheat a mini waffle iron and then grease it.

2. In a bowl, place all ingredients except chocolate chips and lemon zest and beat until well combined.

3. Gently, fold in the chocolate chips and lemon zest.

4. Place ¼ of the mixture into preheated waffle iron and cook for about minutes or until golden brown.

5. Repeat with the remaining mixture.

6. Serve warm.

Nutrition: Calories: Net Carb: 1gFat: 4.8gSaturated Fat: 2.3gCarbohydrates: 1.5gDietary Fiber: 0.5g Sugar: 0.3gProtein: 4.3g

CHAPTER 8:

DESSERT CHAFFLES

24. Plum And Almonds Chaffle

Preparation Time: 15 minutes

Difficulty level: Easy **Cooking Time:** 20 minutes

Servings: 4

Ingredients:

- Cheddar cheese: 1/3 cup

- Egg: 1

- Lemon juice: 1 tbsp.

- Plum: ½ cup puree

- Almond flour: 2 tbsp.

- Baking powder: 1/4 teaspoon

- Ground almonds: 2 tbsp.

- Mozzarella cheese: 1/3 cup

Directions:

1. Mix cheddar cheese, egg, lemon juice, almond flour, plum, almond ground, and baking powder together in a bowl

2. Preheat your waffle iron and grease it

3. In your mini waffle iron, shred half of the Mozzarella cheese Add the mixture to your mini waffle iron Again, shred the remaining Mozzarella cheese on the mixture Cooking till the desired crisp is achieved Make as many chaffles as your mixture and waffle

Nutrition: Calories 145 Net Carbs 0.5 g Total Fat 11.g Saturated Fat 6.6 g Cholesterol 112 mg Sodium 284 g Total Carbs 0.5 g Fiber 0 g Sugar 0.3 g Protein 9.8 g

25. <u>Easy Blueberry Chaffle</u>

Preparation Time: 5 minutes **Difficulty level:** Medium

Cooking Time: 10 minutes

Servings: 2

Ingredients:

- Egg: 2

- Cream cheese: 2 oz.

- Coconut flour: 2 tbsp.

- Swerve/Monk fruit: 4 tsp.

- Baking powder: ½ tsp.

- Vanilla extract: 1 tsp.

- Blueberries: ½ cup

Directions:

1. Take a small mixing bowl and add Swerve/Monk fruit, baking powder, and coconut flour and mix them all well

2. Now add eggs, vanilla extract, and cream cheese, and beat them all together till uniform consistency is achieved

3. Preheat a mini waffle maker if needed and grease it

4. Pour the mixture to the lower plate of the waffle maker

5. Add 3-4 fresh blueberries above the mixture and close the lid

6. Cooking for at least 4 minutes to get the desired crunch

7. Remove the chaffle from the heat

8. Make as many chaffles as your mixture and waffle maker allow

9. Serve with butter or whipped cream that you like!

Nutrition: Calories: 147Net Carb: 2.2gFat: 13gSaturated Fat: 10.7gCarbohydrates: 2.Dietary Fiber: 0.7g Sugar: 1.3gProtein: 4g

26. <u>Sweet And Sour Coconut Chaffles</u>

Preparation Time: 5 minutes **Difficulty level:** Medium

Cooking Time: 20 minutes **Servings:** 4

Ingredients:

- Cheddar cheese: 1/3 cup

- Egg: 1

- Monk fruit sweetener: 2 tsp.

- Lemon juice: 2 tbsp.

- Coconut flour: 2 tbsp.

- Baking powder: 1/4 teaspoon

- Coconut flakes: 2 tbsp.

- Mozzarella cheese: 1/3 cup

Directions:

1. Mix cheddar cheese, egg, coconut flour, coconut flakes, monk fruit sweetener, lemon juice, and baking powder together in a bowl

2. Preheat your waffle iron and grease it

3. In your mini waffle iron, shred half of the Mozzarella cheese

4. Add the mixture to your mini waffle iron

5. Again, shred the remaining Mozzarella cheese on the mixture

6. Cooking till the desired crisp is achieved

7. Make as many chaffles as your mixture and waffle maker allow

8. Sprinkle cinnamon powder on top

Nutrition: Calories: 147Net Carb: 2.2gFat: 13gSaturated Fat: 10.7gCarbohydrates: 2.Dietary Fiber: 0.7g Sugar: 1.3gProtein: 4g

27. <u>Plum Coconut Chaffles</u>

Preparation Time: 5 minutes **Difficulty level:** Medium

Cooking Time: 20 minutes

Servings: 4

Ingredients:

- Cheddar cheese: 1/3 cup

- Egg: 1

- Plum: ½ cup pureed

- Coconut flour: 2 tbsp.

- Baking powder: 1/4 teaspoon

- Coconut flakes: 2 tbsp.

- Mozzarella cheese: 1/3 cup

Directions:

1. Mix cheddar cheese, egg, coconut flour, coconut flakes, plum puree, and baking powder together in a bowl

2. Preheat your waffle iron and grease it

3. In your mini waffle iron, shred half of the Mozzarella cheese

4. Add the mixture to your mini waffle iron

5. Again, shred the remaining Mozzarella cheese on the mixture

6. Cooking till the desired crisp is achieved

7. Make as many chaffles as your mixture and waffle maker allow

Nutrition: Calories: 187Net Carb: 1.8gFat: 14.5gSaturated Fat: 5gCarbohydrates: 4.Dietary Fiber: 3.1g Sugar: 0.4gProtein: 8g

CHAPTER 9:

SAVORY CHAFFLES

RECIPES

28. Cheddar Protein Chaffles

Preparation Time: 15 Minutes

Servings: 8 **Difficulty level:** Easy

Cooking Time: 40 Minutes

Ingredients:

- ½ cup golden flax seeds meal

- ½ cup almond flour

- 2 tablespoons unsweetened whey protein powder

- 1 teaspoon organic baking powder

- Salt and freshly ground black pepper, to taste

- ¾ cup Cheddar cheese, shredded

- 1/3 cup unsweetened almond milk

- 2 tablespoons unsalted butter, melted

- 2 large organic eggs, beaten

Directions:

1. Preheat a mini waffle iron and then grease it.

2. In a large bowl, place flax seeds meal, flour, protein powder and baking powder and mix well.

3. Stir in the Cheddar cheese.

4. In another bowl, place the remaining ingredients and beat until well combined.

5. Add the egg mixture into the bowl with flax seeds meal mixture and mix until well combined.

6. Place desired amount of the mixture into preheated waffle iron and cook for about 4-5 minutes or until golden brown.

7. Repeat with the remaining mixture.

8. Serve warm.

Nutrition: Calories: 187Net Carb: 1.8gFat: 14.5gSaturated Fat: 5gCarbohydrates: 4.Dietary Fiber: 3.1g Sugar: 0.4gProtein: 8g

29. <u>Ground Beef Chaffles</u>

Preparation time: 10 minutes

Cooking Time: 20 Minutes

Difficulty level: Easy

Servings: 2

Ingredients:

- ½ cup cooked grass-fed ground beef

- 3 cooked bacon slices, chopped

- 2 organic eggs

- ½ cup Cheddar cheese, shredded

- ½ cup Mozzarella cheese, shredded

- 2 teaspoons steak seasoning

Directions:

1. Preheat a mini waffle iron and then grease it.

2. In a medium bowl, place all ingredients and mix until well combined.

3. Place ¼ of the mixture into preheated waffle iron and cook for about 4-5 minutes or until golden brown.

4. Repeat with the remaining mixture.

5. Serve warm.

Nutrition: Calories: 214Net Carb: 0.gFat: 12gSaturated Fat: 5.7gCarbohydrates: 0.5gDietary Fiber: g Sugar: 0.2gProtein: 2.1g

30. <u>Italian Seasoning Chaffles</u>

Preparation time: 6 minutes

Cooking Time: 8 Minutes

Difficulty level: Easy

Servings: 2

Ingredients:

- ½ cup Mozzarella cheese, shredded

- 1 tablespoon Parmesan cheese, shredded

- 1 organic egg

- ¾ teaspoon coconut flour

- ¼ teaspoon organic baking powder

- 1/8 teaspoon Italian seasoning

- Pinch of salt

Directions:

1. Preheat a mini waffle iron and then grease it.

2. In a medium bowl, place all ingredients and with a fork, mix until well combined.

3. Place half of the mixture into preheated waffle iron and cook for about 4 minutes or until golden brown.

4. Repeat with the remaining mixture.

5. Serve warm.

Nutrition: Calories: 8et Carb: 1.9gFat: 5gSaturated Fat: 2.6gCarbohydrates: 3.8gDietary Fiber: 1.9g Sugar: 0.6gProtein: 6.5g

31.Lemony Fresh Herbs Chaffles

Preparation Time: 10 Minutes

Servings: 6

Difficulty level: Easy

Cooking Time: 24 Minutes

Ingredients:

- ½ cup ground flaxseed

- 2 organic eggs

- ½ cup goat cheddar cheese, grated

- 2-4 tablespoons plain Greek yogurt

- 1 tablespoon avocado oil

- ½ teaspoon baking soda

- 1 teaspoon fresh lemon juice

- 2 tablespoons fresh chives, minced

- 1 tablespoon fresh basil, minced

- ½ tablespoon fresh mint, minced

- ¼ tablespoon fresh thyme, minced

- ¼ tablespoon fresh oregano, minced

- Salt and freshly ground black pepper, to taste

Directions:

1. Preheat a waffle iron and then grease it.

2. In a medium bowl, place all ingredients and with a fork, mix until well combined.

3. Divide the mixture into 6 portions.

4. Place 1 portion of the mixture into preheated waffle iron and cook for about minutes or until golden brown.

5. Repeat with the remaining mixture.

6. Serve warm.

Nutrition: Calories: 11et Carb: 0.9gFat: 7.9gSaturated Fat: 3gCarbohydrates: 3.7gDietary Fiber: 2.8g Sugar: 0.7gProtein: 6.4g

32. <u>Pork Rind Chaffles</u>

Preparation time: 6 minutes

Difficulty level: Easy

Cooking Time: 10 Minutes

Servings: 2

Ingredients:

- 1 organic egg, beaten

- ½ cup ground pork rinds

- 1/3 cup Mozzarella cheese, shredded

- Pinch of salt

Directions:

1. Preheat a mini waffle iron and then grease it.

2. In a bowl, place all the ingredients and beat until well combined.

3. Place half of the mixture into preheated waffle iron and cook for about 5 minutes or until golden brown.

4. Repeat with the remaining mixture.

5. Serve warm.

Nutrition: Calories: 91Net Carb: 0.3gFat: 5.9gSaturated Fat: 2.3gCarbohydrates: 0.3gDietary Fiber: 0g Sugar: 0.2gProtein: 9.2g

33. <u>Salmon Chaffles</u>

Preparation time: 6 minutes

Difficulty level: Easy

Cooking Time: 10 Minutes

Servings: 2

Ingredients:

- 1 large egg

- ½ cup shredded mozzarella

- 1 Tbsp cream cheese

- 2 slices salmon

- 1 Tbsp everything bagel seasoning

Directions:

1. Turn on waffle maker to heat and oil it with cooking spray.

2. Beat egg in a bowl, then add ½ cup mozzarella.

3. Pour half of the mixture into the waffle maker and cook for 4 minutes.

4. Remove and repeat with remaining mixture.

5. Let chaffles cool, then spread cream cheese, sprinkle with seasoning, and top with salmon.

Nutrition: Carbs: 3 g ;Fat: 10 g ;Protein: 5 g ;Calories: 201

34. <u>Chaffle Katsu Sandwich</u>

Preparation time: 10 minutes

Difficulty level: Easy

Cooking Time: 00 Minutes

Servings: 2

Ingredients:

- For the chicken:

- ¼ lb boneless and skinless chicken thigh

- ⅛ tsp salt

- ⅛ tsp black pepper

- ½ cup almond flour

- 1 egg

- 3 oz unflavored pork rinds

- 2 cup vegetable oil for deep frying

- For the brine:

- 2 cup of water

- 1 Tbsp salt

- For the sauce:

- 2 Tbsp sugar-free ketchup

- 1½ Tbsp Worcestershire Sauce

- 1 Tbsp oyster sauce

- 1 tsp swerve/monk fruit

- For the chaffle:

- 2 egg

- 1 cup shredded mozzarella cheese

Directions:

1. Add brine ingredients in a large mixing bowl.

2. Add chicken and brine for 1 hour.

3. Pat chicken dry with a paper towel. Sprinkle with salt and pepper. Set aside.

4. Mix ketchup, oyster sauce, Worcestershire sauce, and swerve in a small mixing bowl.

5. Pulse pork rinds in a food processor, making fine crumbs.

6. Fill one bowl with flour, a second bowl with beaten eggs, and a third with crushed pork rinds.

7. Dip and coat each thigh in: flour, eggs, crushed pork rinds. Transfer on holding a plate.

8. Add oil to cover ½ inch of frying pan. Heat to 375°F.

9. Once oil is hot, reduce heat to medium and add chicken. Cooking time depends on the chicken thickness.

10. Transfer to a drying rack.

11. Turn on waffle maker to heat and oil it with cooking spray.

12. Beat egg in a small bowl.

13. Place ⅛ cup of cheese on waffle maker, then add¼ of the egg mixture and top with ⅛ cup of cheese.

14. Cook for 3-4 minutes.

15. Repeat for remaining batter.

16. Top chaffles with chicken katsu, 1 Tbsp sauce, and another piece of chaffle.

Nutrition: Carbs: 12 g ;Fat: 1 g ;Protein: 2 g ;Calories: 57

35. <u>Parmesan Garlic Chaffle</u>

Preparation time: 6 minutes

Cooking Time: 5 Minutes

Difficulty level: Easy

Servings: 2

Ingredients:

- 1 Tbsp fresh garlic minced

- 2 Tbsp butter 1-oz cream cheese, cubed

- 2 Tbsp almond flour

- 1 tsp baking soda

- 2 large eggs 1 tsp dried chives

- ½ cup parmesan cheese, shredded

- ¾ cup mozzarella cheese, shredded

Directions:

1. Heat cream cheese and butter in a saucepan over medium-low until melted.

2. Add garlic and cook, stirring, for minutes.

3. Turn on waffle maker to heat and oil it with cooking spray.

4. In a small mixing bowl, whisk together flour and baking soda, then set aside.

5. In a separate bowl, beat eggs for 1 minute 30 seconds on high, then add in cream cheese mixture and beat for 60 seconds more.

6. Add flour mixture, chives, and cheeses to the bowl and stir well.

7. Add ¼ cup batter to waffle maker.

8. Close and cook for 4 minutes, until golden brown.

9. Repeat for remaining batter.

10. Add favorite toppings and serve.

Nutrition: Carbs: 5 g ;Fat: 33 g ;Protein: 19 g ;Calories: 385

36. <u>Garlic Cheese Chaffle Bread Sticks</u>

Preparation time: 10 minutes

Servings: 8

Cooking Time: 5 Minutes

Difficulty level: Easy

Ingredients:

- 1 medium egg

- ½ cup mozzarella cheese, grated

- 2 Tbsp almond flour

- ½ tsp garlic powder

- ½ tsp oregano

- ½ tsp salt

- For the toppings:

- 2 Tbsp butter, unsalted softened

- ½ tsp garlic powder

- ¼ cup grated mozzarella cheese

- 2 tsp dried oregano for sprinkling

Directions:

1. Turn on waffle maker to heat and oil it with cooking spray.

2. Beat egg in a bowl.

3. Add mozzarella, garlic powder, flour, oregano, and salt, and mix.

4. Spoon half of the batter into the waffle maker.

5. Close and cook for minutes. Remove cooked chaffle.

6. Repeat with remaining batter.

7. Place chaffles on a tray and preheat the grill.

8. Mix butter with garlic powder and spread over the chaffles.

9. Sprinkle mozzarella over top and cook under the broiler for 2-3 minutes, until cheese has melted.

Nutrition: Carbs: 1 g ;Fat: 7 g ;Protein: 4 g ;Calories: 74

CHAPTER 10:

FESTIVE CHAFFLE

RECIPES

37. Chaffle Cream Cake

Preparation Time: 10 minutes **ervings:** 8 **Difficulty level:**

Medium **Cooking Time:** 30 Minutes

Ingredients:

- Chaffle

- 4 oz. cream cheese

- 4 eggs

- 1 tablespoon butter, melted

- 1 teaspoon vanilla extract

- ½ teaspoon cinnamon

- 1 tablespoon sweetener

- 4 tablespoons coconut flour

- 1 tablespoon almond flour

- 1 ½ teaspoons baking powder

- 1 tablespoon coconut flakes (sugar-free)

- 1 tablespoon walnuts, chopped

- Frosting

- 2 oz. cream cheese

- 2 tablespoons butter

- 2 tablespoons sweetener

- ½ teaspoon vanilla

Directions:

1. Combine all the chaffle ingredients except coconut flakes and walnuts in a blender.

2. Blend until smooth.

3. Plug in your waffle maker.

4. Add some of the mixture to the waffle maker.

5. Cook for 3 minutes.

6. Repeat steps until the remaining batter is used. While letting the chaffles cool, make the frosting by combining all the ingredients.

7. Use a mixer to combine and turn frosting into fluffy consistency.

8. Spread the frosting on top of the chaffles.

Nutrition: Calories127 Total Fat 13.7g Saturated Fat 9 g Cholesterol .9mg Sodium 107.3mg Potassium 457 mg Total Carbohydrate 5.5g Dietary Fiber 1.3g Protein 5.3g Total Sugars 1.5

38. <u>Crunchy Coconut Chaffles Cake</u>

Preparation time: 5 minutes **Difficulty level:** Medium

Cooking Time: 15 Minutes **Servings:** 2

Ingredients:

- 4 large eggs 1 cup shredded cheese

- 2 tbsps. coconut cream

- 2 tbsps. coconut flour.

- 1 tsp. stevia

- TOPPING

- 1 cup heavy cream 8 oz. raspberries

- 4 oz. blueberries

- 2 oz. cherries

Directions:

1. Make 4 thin round chaffles with the chaffle ingredients. Once chaffles are cooked, set in layers on a plate.

2. Spread heavy cream in each layer.

3. Top with raspberries then blueberries and cherries.

4. Serve and enjoy!

Nutrition: Protein: 21% 67 kcal Fat: 72% 230 kcal Carbohydrates: 7% 21 kcal

39. <u>Holidays Chaffles</u>

Preparation time: 5 minutes

Cooking Time: 5 minutes

Servings: 2

Difficulty level: Medium

Ingredients:

- 1 cup egg whites

- 2 tsps. coconut flour

- ½ tsp. Vanilla

- 1 tsp. baking powder

- 1 tsp. baking soda

- 1/8 tsp cinnamon powder

- 1 cup mozzarella cheese, grated

- TOPPING

- Cranberries

- keto Chocolate sauce

Directions:

1. Make 4 minutes chaffles from the chaffle ingredients.

2. Top with chocolate sauce and cranberries

3. Serve hot and enjoy!

Nutrition: Protein: 38% 133 kcal Fat: 57% 201 kcal

Carbohydrates: 5% 18 kcal

40. <u>Bacon, Egg & Avocado Chaffle Sandwich</u>

Preparation time: 10 minutes

Difficulty level: Medium

Cooking Time: 10 Minutes

Servings: 2

Ingredients:

- Cooking spray

- 4 slices bacon

- 2 eggs

- ½ avocado, mashed

- 4 basic chaffles

- 2 leaves lettuce

Directions:

1. Coat your skillet with cooking spray.

2. Cook the bacon until golden and crisp.

3. Transfer into a paper towel lined plate.

4. Crack the eggs into the same pan and cook until firm.

5. Flip and cook until the yolk are set.

6. Spread the avocado on the chaffle.

7. Top with lettuce, egg and bacon.

8. Top with another chaffle.

Nutrition: Calories 372 Total Fat 30.1g Saturated Fat 8.6g Cholesterol 205mg Sodium 3mg Total Carbohydrate 5.4g Dietary Fiber 3.4g Total Sugars 0.6g Protein 20.6g Potassium 524mg

CHAPTER 11:

SPECIAL CHAFFLE

RECIPES

41.Super Easy Chocolate Chaffles

Preparation time: 10 minutes

Difficulty level: Medium

Cooking Time:5 minutes

Servings: 2

Ingredients:

- 1/4 cup unsweetened chocolate chips

- 1 egg

- 2 tbsps. almond flour

- 1/2 cup mozzarella cheese

- 1 tbsp. Greek yogurts

- 1/2 tsp. baking powder

- 1 tsp. stevia

Directions:

1. Switch on your square chaffle maker.

2. Spray the waffle maker with cooking spray.

3. Mix together all recipe ingredients in a mixing bowl.

4. Spoon batter in a greased waffle maker and make two chaffles.

5. Once chaffles are cooked, remove from the maker.

6. Serve with coconut cream, shredded chocolate, and nuts on top.

7. Enjoy!

Nutrition: Protein: 35% 59 kcal Fat: 59% 99 kcal Carbohydrates: 6% 10 kcal

42. **Pumpkin Cheesecake Chaffle**

Preparation time: 10 minutes

Difficulty level: Medium

Cooking Time: 15 Minutes

Servings: 2

Ingredients:

- For chaffle:

- 1 egg

- 1/2 tsp vanilla

- 1/2 tsp baking powder, gluten-free

- 1/4 tsp pumpkin spice

- 1 tsp cream cheese, softened

- 2 tsp heavy cream

- 1 tbsp Swerve

- 1 tbsp almond flour

- 2 tsp pumpkin puree

- 1/2 cup mozzarella cheese, shredded

- For filling:

- 1/4 tsp vanilla

- 1 tbsp Swerve

- 2 tbsp cream cheese

Directions:

1. Preheat your mini waffle maker.

2. In a small bowl, mix all chaffle ingredients. Spray waffle maker with cooking spray. Pour half batter in the hot waffle maker and cook for 3-5 minutes. Repeat with the remaining batter.

3. In a small bowl, combine all filling ingredients. Spread filling mixture between two chaffles and place in the fridge for 10 minutes. Serve and enjoy.

Nutrition: Calories 107Fat 7.2 carbohydrates 5 sugar 0.7 protein 6.7 cholesterol 93 mg

43. <u>Churro Chaffle</u>

Preparation time: 10 minutes

Difficulty level: Medium

Cooking Time: 8 Minutes **Servings:** 2

Ingredients:

- 1 egg

- ½ cup mozzarella cheese, shredded

- ½ teaspoon cinnamon

- 2 tablespoons sweetener

Directions:

1. Turn on your waffle iron.

2. Beat the egg in a bowl.

3. Stir in the cheese.

4. Pour half of the mixture into the waffle maker.

5. Cover the waffle iron.

6. Cook for 4 minutes.

7. While waiting, mix the cinnamon and sweetener in a bowl.

8. Open the device and soak the waffle in the cinnamon mixture.

9. Repeat the steps with the remaining batter.

Nutrition: Calories   Total   Fat   6.9g   Saturated   Fat 2.9g   Cholesterol   171mg   Sodium   147mg   Potassium 64mg   Total Carbohydrate 5.8g Dietary Fiber 2.6g Protein 9.6g Total Sugars 0.4g

CHAPTER 12:

OTHER KETO CHAFFLES

44. Bacon Jalapeno Popper Chaffle

Preparation time: 10 minutes **Difficulty level:** Easy

Cooking Time: 10 Minutes **Servings:** 2

Ingredients:

- 4 slices bacon (diced)

- 3 eggs

- 3 tbsp coconut flour

- 1 tsp baking powder

- ¼ tsp salt

- ½ tsp oregano

- A pinch of onion powder

- A pinch of garlic powder

- ½ cup cream cheese

- 1 cup shredded cheddar cheese

- 2 jalapeno pepper (deseeded and chopped)

- ½ cup sour cream

Directions:

1. Plug the waffle maker to preheat it and spray it with a non-stick cooking spray.

2. Heat up a frying pan over medium to high heat. Add the bacon and saute until the bacon is brown and crispy.

3. Use a slotted spoon to transfer the bacon to a paper towel lined plate to drain.

4. In a mixing bowl, combine the coconut flour, baking powder, salt, oregano, onion and garlic.

5. In another mixing bowl, whisk together the egg and cream cheese until well combined.

6. Add the cheddar cheese and mix. Pour in the flour mixture and mix until you form a smooth batter.

7. Pour an appropriate amount of the batter into the waffle maker and spread the batter to the edges to cover all the holes on the waffle maker.

8. Close the waffle maker and cook for about 5 minutes or according to waffle maker's settings.

9. After the cooking cycle, use a plastic or silicone utensil to remove the chaffle from the waffle maker.

10. Repeat step 7 to 9 until you have cooked all the batter into chaffles.

11. Serve warm and top with sour cream, crispy bacon and jalapeno slices.

Nutrition: Fat 51g 65% Carbohydrate 13.5g 5% Sugars 2.1g Protein 30.6g

45. Zucchini Bacon Chaffles

Preparation time: 9 minutes

Difficulty level: Easy

Cooking Time: 12 Minutes **Servings:** 2

Ingredients:

- 1 cup grated zucchini

- 1 tbsp bacon bits (finely chopped)

- ¼ cup shredded mozzarella cheese

- ½ cup shredded parmesan

- ½ tsp salt or to taste

- ½ tsp ground black pepper or to taste

- ½ tsp onion powder

- ¼ tsp nutmeg 2 eggs

Directions:

1. Add ¼ tsp salt to the grated zucchini and let it sit for about 5 minutes.

2. Put the grated zucchini in a clean towel and squeeze out excess water.

3. Plug the waffle maker and preheat it. Spray it with non-stick spray.

4. Break the eggs into a mixing bowl and beat.

5. Add the grated zucchini, bacon bit, nutmeg, onion powder, pepper, salt and mozzarella.

6. Add ¾ of the parmesan cheese. You have to set aside some parmesan cheese.

7. Mix until the ingredients are well combined.

8. Fill the preheated waffle maker with the batter and spread out the batter to the edge to cover all the holes on the waffle maker.

9. Close the waffle maker lid and cook until the chaffle is golden brown and crispy. The zucchini chaffle may take longer than other chaffles to get crispy.

10. After the baking cycle, use a plastic or silicone utensil to remove the chaffle from the waffle maker.

11. Repeat step 8 to 10 until you have cooked all the batter into chaffles.

12. Serve and enjoy.

Nutrition: Fat 6g 17% Carbohydrate 4.7g 2% Sugars 1.6g Protein 20.4g

46. <u>Bacon Chaffles With Herb Dip</u>

Preparation time: 9 minutes

Difficulty level: Easy

Time: 10 Minutes

Cooking Time: 25 Minutes

Servings: 2

Ingredients:

- Chaffles

- 1 organic egg, beaten

- ½ cup Swiss/Gruyere cheese blend, shredded

- 2 tablespoons cooked bacon pieces

- 1 tablespoon jalapeño pepper, chopped

- Dip

- ¼ cup heavy cream

- ¼ teaspoon fresh dill, minced

- Pinch of ground black pepper

Directions:

1. Preheat a mini waffle iron and then grease it.

2. For chaffles: In a medium bowl, put all ingredients and mix well.

3. Place half of the mixture into preheated waffle iron and cook for about 5 minutes.

4. Repeat with the remaining mixture.

5. Meanwhile, for dip: in a bowl, mix together the cream and stevia.

6. Serve warm chaffles alongside the dip.

Nutrition: Calories 210 Net Carbs 2.2 g Total Fat 13 g Saturated Fat 9.7 g Cholesterol 132 mg Sodium 164 mg Total Carbs 2.3 g Fiber 0.1 g Sugar 0.7 g Protein 11.9 g

47. <u>Shirataki Rice Chaffle</u>

Preparation time: 8 minutes **Difficulty level:** Easy

Cooking Time: 20 Minutes **Servings:** 2

Ingredients:

- 2 tbsp almond flour

- ½ tsp oregano

- 1 bag of shirataki rice

- 1 tsp baking powder

- 1 cup shredded cheddar cheese

- 2 eggs (beaten)

Directions:

1. Rinse the shirataki rice with warm water for about 30 seconds and rinse it.

2. Plug the waffle maker to preheat it and spray it with a non-stick cooking spray.

3. In a mixing bowl, combine the rinsed rice, almond flour, baking powder, oregano and shredded cheese. Add the eggs and mix until the ingredients are well combined.

4. Fill the waffle maker with an appropriate amount of the batter and spread out the batter to the edges to cover all the holes on the waffle maker.

5. Close the waffle make and cook for about minutes or according to you waffle maker's settings.

6. After the cooking cycle, use a silicone or plastic utensil to remove the chaffles from the waffle maker.

7. Repeat step 4 to 6 until you have cooked all the batter into chaffles.

8. Serve and enjoy.

Nutrition: Fat 13.2g   17%   Carbohydrate 2g   1% Sugars 0.3g Protein 10.6g

48. <u>Eggnog Chaffle</u>

Preparation time: 9 minutes

Difficulty level: Easy

Cooking Time: 5 Minutes

Servings: 2

Ingredients:

- 2 tbsp coconut flour

- ½ tsp baking powder

- 1 tsp cinnamon

- 2 tbsp cream cheese

- 2 tsp swerve

- 1/8 tsp salt

- 1/8 tsp nutmeg

- 1 egg (beaten)

- 4 tbsp keto eggnog

- Eggnog Filling:

- 4 tbsp keto eggnog

- ¼ tsp vanilla extract

- ¼ cup heavy cream

- 2 tsp granulated swerve

- 1/8 tsp nutmeg

Directions:

1. Plug the waffle maker to preheat it and spray it with a non-stick cooking spray.

2. Combine the coconut flour, baking powder, swerve, salt, cinnamon and nutmeg in a mixing bowl.

3. In another mixing bowl, whisk together the eggnog, cream cheese and egg.

4. Pour in the egg mixture into the flour mixture and mix until the ingredients are well combined.

5. Fill the waffle maker with an appropriate amount of the batter. Spread out the batter to cover all the holes on the waffle maker.

6. Close the waffle maker and cook for about 5 minutes or according to your waffle maker's settings.

7. After the baking cycle, remove the chaffle from the waffle maker with a plastic or silicone utensil.

8. Repeat step 5 to 7 until you have cooked all the batter into chaffles.

9. For the eggnog cream, whisk together the cream cheese, heavy cream, vanilla and eggnog. Add the swerve and nutmeg; mix until the ingredients are well combined.

10. Top the chaffles with the eggnog cream and enjoy

Nutrition: Fat 12.1g 16% Carbohydrate 16.1g 6% Sugars 3.4g Protein 6.9g

CHAPTER 13:

CHAFFLE MEAT RECIPES

49. Pork Loin Chaffle Sandwich

Preparation time: 10 minutes

Difficulty level: Easy

Cooking Time: 15 Minutes

Servings: 2

Ingredients:

- 4 eggs

- 1 cup grated mozzarella cheese

- 1 cup grated parmesan cheese

- Salt and pepper to taste

- 2 tablespoons cream cheese

- 6 tablespoons coconut flour

- 2 teaspoons baking powder

- Pork loin 2 tablespoons olive oil

- 1 pound pork loin Salt and pepper to taste

- 2 cloves garlic, minced

- 1 tablespoon freshly chopped thyme

- Other 2 tablespoons cooking spray to brush the waffle maker 4 lettuce leaves for serving

- 4 slices of tomato for serving

- ¼ cup sugar-free mayonnaise for serving

Directions:

1. Preheat the waffle maker.

2. Add the eggs, mozzarella cheese, parmesan cheese, salt and pepper, cream cheese, coconut flour and baking powder to a bowl.

3. Mix until combined.

4. Brush the heated waffle maker with cooking spray and add a few tablespoons of the batter.

5. Close the lid and cook for about 7 minutes depending on your waffle maker.

6. Meanwhile, heat the olive oil in a nonstick frying pan and season the pork loin with salt and pepper, minced garlic and freshly chopped thyme.

7. Cook the pork loin for about 5–minutes on each side.

8. Cut each chaffle in half and add some mayonnaise, lettuce leaf, tomato slice and sliced pork loin on one half.

9. Cover the sandwich with the other chaffle half and serve.

Nutrition: Calories 7 fat 52.7 g, carbs 11.3 g, sugar 0.8 g, Protein 47.4 g, sodium 513 mg

50. <u>Chicken Parmesan Chaffles</u>

Preparation time: 10 minutes

Difficulty level: Easy

Cooking Time: 8 Minutes **Servings:** 2

Ingredients:

- 1/3 cup chicken

- 1 egg

- 1/3 cup mozzarella cheese

- 1/4 tsp basil

- 1/4 garlic

- 2 tbsp tomato sauce

- 2 tbsp Mozzarella cheese

Directions:

1. Heat up your Dash mini waffle maker.

2. In a small bowl, mix the egg, cooked chicken, basil, garlic, and Mozzarella Cheese.

3. Add 1/2 of the batter into your mini waffle maker and cook for 4 minutes. If they are still a bit uncooked, leave it cooking for another 2 minutes. Then cook the rest of the batter to make a second chaffle and then cook the third chaffle. After cooking, remove from the pan and let sit for 2 minutes.

4. Top with 1-2 tablespoons sauce on each chicken parmesan chaffle. Then sprinkle 1-2 tablespoon mozzarella cheese.

5. Put chaffles in the oven or a toaster oven at 400 degrees and cook until the cheese is melted.

Nutrition: (per serving):Calories: 185kcal ;Carbohydrates:2g ;Protein: 14g;Fat: 13g ;Saturated Fat:6g ;Cholesterol:122mg ;Sodium:254mg ;Potassium: 66mg ;Sugar: 1g ;Vitamin A: 3IU ;Calcium: 181mg ;Iron: 1mg

CONCLUSION

I n the low-carb world, the word 'CHAFFLE' appeared and took the social media by storm. The waffle maker became the need of every keto kitchen and individuals following ketogenic diet found their new love. This new addition in the keto diet is not only healthy but the possibilities to experiment with new recipes are countless.

Furthermore, it has also made it easy for keto followers to follow their diet and controlling their cravings for flour based foods. In simple words, chaffles are the low-carb waffles – they are called chaffle because cheese is used as their base ingredient. Cheese and waffle by combining these words you will get the delicious chaffles.

Another benefit that we offer? We explain routines that you can do for yourself to make this diet last longer for you and to benefit your body better as a result. Routines are very important and can be a big help to your body but also your spirit and your mind.

This will help you utilize the diet better, and you will be able to improve with it as well as have it become easier for you to handle. You want to stay healthy and make sure that your body is able to do what it needs to.

As with anything, we have put a strong emphasis on the fact that if anything feels wrong or unnatural, you will need to see a doctor to make sure that you are safe and that your body can handle this diet. Use the knowledge in this book to have amazing recipes and learn how to prepare amazing meals for you.

How to Clean and Maintain the Waffle Maker

Make sure that it is not hot before you clean the waffle or chaffle maker. But clean it as soon as it is cool enough.

1. Use a damp cloth or paper towel for wiping away the crumbs.
2. Soak up the excess oil drips on your grid plates.
3. Wipe the exterior with the damp cloth or paper towel.
4. Pour a few drops of cooking oil on the batter to remove the stubborn batter drips. Wipe it away after this.
5. You can wash the cooking plates in soapy warm water. Rinse them clean.

6. Ensure that the waffle maker is completely dry before storing it.

Waffle Maker Maintenance Tips

Remember these simple tips and your waffle maker will serve you for a long time.

- Instruction manual should be well read before you use it for the first time.
- Only a light cooking oil coating is required for nonstick waffle makers.
- Grease the grid with only a little amount of oil if you see the waffles sticking.
- Never use metal or sharp tools to scrape off the batter or to remove the cooked waffles. You may end up scratching the surface and damaging it.
- Do not submerge your electric waffle maker in water.

Chaffles can be frozen and processed, so a large proportion can be made and stored for quick and extremely fast meals. If you don't have a waffle maker, just cook the mixture like a pancake in a frying pan, or even cooler, in a fryer-pan. They won't get all the fluffy sides to achieve like you're using a waffle maker, but they're definitely going to taste great.

Depending on which cheese you choose, the carbs and net calorie number can shift a little bit. However, in general, whether you use real, whole milk cheese, chaffles are completely carb-free.

For up to a month, chaffles will be frozen. However, defrosting them absorbs plenty of moist, which makes it difficult to get their crisp again. Chaffles are rich in fat and moderate in protein and low in carb. Chaffle is a very well established and popular technique to hold people on board.

And the chaffles are more durable and better than most forms of keto bread. "What a high-carb diet you may be desirous of. A nonstick waffle maker is something that makes life easier, and it's a trade-off that's happy to embrace for our wellbeing.

CPSIA information can be obtained
at www.ICGtesting.com
Printed in the USA
BVHW091105170521
607543BV00005B/471